PUBLIC LIBRARY DISTRICT OF COLUMBIA

W9-CNH-441

Zoom In On
WATER AND
SEWAGE SYSTEMS

Kathy Furgang

E | **Enslow P**
101 W. 23rd Str
Suite 240
New York, NY 1(
USA
enslow.c

WORDS TO KNOW

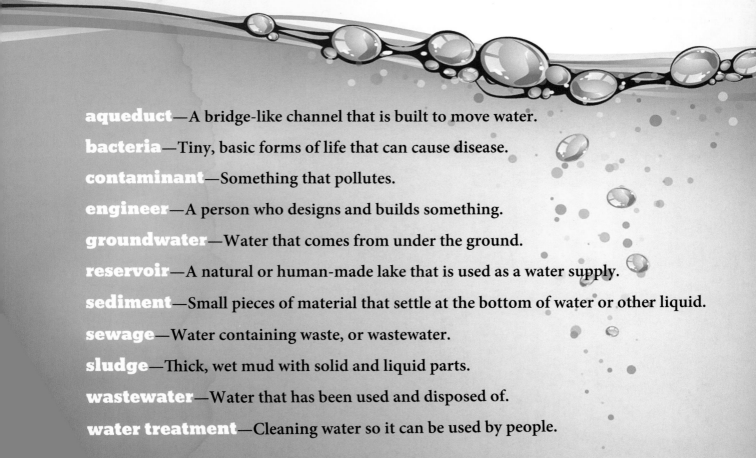

aqueduct—A bridge-like channel that is built to move water.

bacteria—Tiny, basic forms of life that can cause disease.

contaminant—Something that pollutes.

engineer—A person who designs and builds something.

groundwater—Water that comes from under the ground.

reservoir—A natural or human-made lake that is used as a water supply.

sediment—Small pieces of material that settle at the bottom of water or other liquid.

sewage—Water containing waste, or wastewater.

sludge—Thick, wet mud with solid and liquid parts.

wastewater—Water that has been used and disposed of.

water treatment—Cleaning water so it can be used by people.

CONTENTS

Words to Know 2

1 Water Long Ago 5

2 How Water Gets to Us 9

3 What Happens After Water
Is Used? 14

4 How Water Is Used 19

Activity 22

Learn More 24

Index 24

Today, people no longer have to live close to water sources because water can be sent to our homes.

Water Long Ago

What can you do to get clean, fresh water to drink or bathe with? Simply turn on the faucet! But how does the water get to your faucet, ready to use whenever you need it? That answer has to do with science and technology. But it was not always so easy to get clean water.

Throughout history, people have built their homes around rivers and other water sources. After all, we need water to survive. People also came up with ways to get fresh water from underground sources. But when groundwater is collected, the sand has to be removed. The water has to be cleaned. Getting clean water is difficult!

Keeping It Clean

Why is it so important for water to be clean? Dirty water can make people very sick. Bacteria in dirty water can even kill people.

As time has gone on, people have found ways to move water over long distances. Long ago, people in Rome built water channels called aqueducts. These structures carried water to people who lived farther away from water sources. They used it to drink and water their crops.

The aqueducts from ancient Rome are no longer used, but some are still standing.

Today, complicated systems bring clean water to people in cities and towns all over the world. Engineers design and build these systems, called water treatment plants. Other systems clean water that has already been used. These systems are called wastewater treatment systems.

Early Engineers

Some aqueducts were tunnels connecting a higher area of ground to a lower area. In ancient Rome, aqueducts were some of the first large-scale modern engineering projects. Water was moved across rivers and valleys using gravity.

How Water Gets to Us

Reservoirs are important water sources. In a reservoir, water is collected and then used later. Some reservoirs are natural lakes or rivers. Other reservoirs are made by people. Some water comes from underground sources called aquifers.

Water that comes from these sources is not clean enough to drink right away. First, pipes take the collected water to treatment plants to be cleaned. The

Reservoirs collect rainwater that can be cleaned and used later. This reservoir is in New York City.

water goes through several large tanks. Each one does a different job.

From Tanks to Homes

First, the water sits in tanks so large pieces of sediment and other materials can settle to the bottom and later be removed. Then the water goes to tanks where even smaller pieces are filtered out. After being pumped

Getting Water Clean

There are many ways to remove materials from water at treatment plants. One way is to filter the water. The water flows through a screen like a coffee filter. The water passes through the screen, but tiny pieces of material are caught by the screen.

Water treatment plants contain many different tanks for cleaning water.

to other tanks, chemicals are added to the water to make it safe to drink. Finally, the water is pumped out of the plant.

After leaving the plant, the water is pumped through thick, large pipes. These pipes may take the water to large water towers. The towers are high above the ground so the water can easily flow downward. The water then goes through underground pipes until it finally arrives at people's homes.

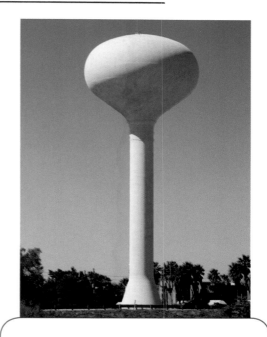

Water can be stored in large towers like this one. From here, it goes through pipes to homes and businesses.

13

What Happens After Water Is Used?

After water is cleaned, it can be delivered to homes and businesses. After water is used, it becomes wastewater. Pipes take this used water and waste, or sewage, out of homes and businesses. They drain into larger pipes and the wastewater is brought to treatment centers to be cleaned.

Water is constantly being recycled. After the water is used, it is cleaned and reused. The cleaning

A wastewater treatment plant

The scrapers push sludge toward the middle of the tank where it can be removed.

process is very important. If all contaminants are not removed, the dirty water will return to water sources such as rivers or lakes. It will pollute the environment. It will make drinking water more difficult to clean when it goes to treatment plants to be used.

Treating Water

Water at wastewater treatment plants goes through the same kinds of stages that it does in water treatment plants. First, the water is screened to remove large objects that have been flushed away by people. Pieces of glass, plastics, or papers are removed at this stage. Solid wastes are removed in the next stage. The solids that settle to the bottom of a tank are called sludge. The tanks have large scrapers that move around the tank in a circle. The scrapers push the sludge toward the center of the tank where they are pumped away and separated from the water.

Helping the Public

People who design and build wastewater treatment plants are civil engineers. This type of engineer works on projects that affect the public. This includes building bridges, dams, canals, and large facilities for bringing resources to the public.

Final Steps

Even though large and small materials have been removed from the wastewater, you wouldn't want to drink it yet! The water still needs to be cleaned. Air is pumped into the water tanks. This breaks down any contaminants that might have gotten through the filters. Then, the water sits and settles. Any remaining sludge is then separated and removed from the water. Finally, the water can be filtered into a river and back into the water supply.

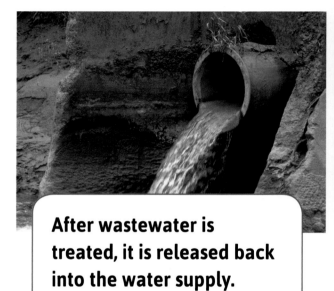

After wastewater is treated, it is released back into the water supply.

How Water Is Used

Water is not just for drinking. Water is needed to grow food. It is needed to feed farm animals. Big businesses and factories use large amounts of water. Each place has strict rules about how to clean their wastewater. Some businesses use dangerous chemicals. If those chemicals get into rivers and lakes, they can kill living things there. The chemicals can get into our water supply.

A Valuable Resource

The average American family uses more than 300 gallons of water in their home every day. Most of that water is used indoors. And only about 15 percent of that water is used from faucets for drinking water. The rest is used for activities such as showering, flushing the toilet, and washing clothes. About 13 percent of that water is a result of water leaks! That's why saving water is important. Saving water will mean there will be enough for everyone.

People need water for many reasons.

How Much Water Do We Use?

Each activity we do at home uses a different amount of water. Check out the chart to see how many gallons each activity uses.

Activity	Gallons of Water Used
Bathing	36
Showering	2 per minute
Flushing Toilet	3
Clothes Washer	25
Dishwasher	Up to 16

ACTIVITY
TRACKING YOUR WATER USE

How do you use water every day? Use the chart below to help you keep track. Write the activity in the left column. Then mark each day you do that activity. A few examples are given to get you started.

Activity	Mon	Tues	Wed	Thurs	Fri	Sat	Sun
Brush teeth							
Take a bath							

Estimate how much water each of the above activities uses.

Washing the car can use up a lot of water!

LEARN MORE

Books

Linde, Barbara. *What Is Wastewater?* New York, NY: Gareth Stevens, 2016.

Mulder, Michelle. *Every Last Drop: Bringing Clean Water Home*. Cluster, WA: Orca, 2014.

Yomtov, Nel. *Water/Wastewater Engineer.* North Mankato, MN: Cherry Lake Publishing, 2015.

Websites

US Environmental Protection Agency
www3.epa.gov/safewaer/kids/kids_k-3.html
www3.epa.gov/safewater/kids/kids_4-8.html
This website provides activities for children in grades K-3 and 4-8 to help them learn about the water cycle and water usage.

USGS
water.usgs.gov/edu/wwvisit.html
This article explains the process of wastewater treatment.

INDEX

aqueducts, 6, 8

clean water, 6–8

contaminants, 16

engineers, 8, 17

groundwater, 6

how much water we use, 20–21

pollution, 16, 19

reservoirs, 9

sediment, 11

sewage, 14

sludge, 17

wastewater treatment, 8, 16–18

water treatment, 8, 9–13

Published in 2018 by Enslow Publishing, LLC
101 W. 23rd Street, Suite 240 New York, NY 10011

Copyright © 2018 by Enslow Publishing, LLC
All rights reserved.

No part of this book may be reproduced by any means without the written permission of the publisher.

Library of Congress Cataloging-in-Publication Data

Names: Furgang, Kathy, author.
Title: Zoom in on water and sewage systems / Kathy Furgang.
Description: New York, NY : Enslow Publishing, 2018. | Series: Zoom in on engineering | Includes bibliographical references and index.
Identifiers: LCCN 2017003030| ISBN 9780766087149 (library-bound) | ISBN 9780766088405 (pbk.) | ISBN 9780766088344 (6-pack)
Subjects: LCSH: Water-supply—Juvenile literature. | Sewerage—Juvenile literature.
Classification: LCC TD348 .F87 2018 | DDC 628.2—dc23
LC record available at https://lccn.loc.gov/2017003030

Printed in the United States of America

To Our Readers: We have done our best to make sure all websites in this book were active and appropriate when we went to press. However, the author and the publisher have no control over and assume no liability for the material available on those websites or on any websites they may link to. Any comments or suggestions can be sent by e-mail to customerservice@enslow.com.

Photo Credits: Cover, p. 1 (inset) lucky78/Shutterstock.com; cover, p. 1 (background) wuttichai janglab/Shutterstock.com; pp. 2, 3, 22, and4me/Shutterstock.com; p. 4 Teresa Short/Moment Open/Getty Images; p. 7 PukkaInc/Shutterstock.com; p. 10 Francois Roux/Shutterstock.com; pp. 12, 15, 16 Kekyalyaynen/Shutterstock.com; p. 13 Steven Hockney/Shutterstock.com; p. 18 Universal Images Group/Getty Images; p. 20 badbanner/Shutterstock.com; p. 23 Anurak Pongpatimet/Shutterstock.com; graphic elements (faucet) kelttt/Shutterstock.com; (water drop) phipatbig/Shutterstock.com.